SUPER SUNDAY

ACTIVITY BOOK

ARIE VAN DE GRAAFF

SUPER SUNDAY
ACTIVITY BOOK

ISBN 13: 978-1-4621-3825-8

Published by CFI, an imprint of Cedar Fort, Inc.
2373 W. 700 S., Springville, UT 84663
Distributed by Cedar Fort, Inc., www.cedarfort.com

Cover and interior layout and design by Shawnda T. Craig
Cover design © 2020 Cedar Fort, Inc.

Printed in the United States of America

10 9 8 7 6 5 4 3 2 1

Printed on acid-free paper

SABBATH DAY ACTIVITIES

Whether it is reading together as a family, taking treats to a neighbor, visiting with faraway family, or enjoying a family meal, there are lots of things you can do on a Sunday. There are also five similar things in these four pictures. Can you find them?

FAMILY PRAYER

This family knows the value of prayer before dinner. Can you find the hidden objects in this picture?

ALMA TEACHES CORIANTON

Can you find ten differences between these two pictures of Alma and his son Corianton?

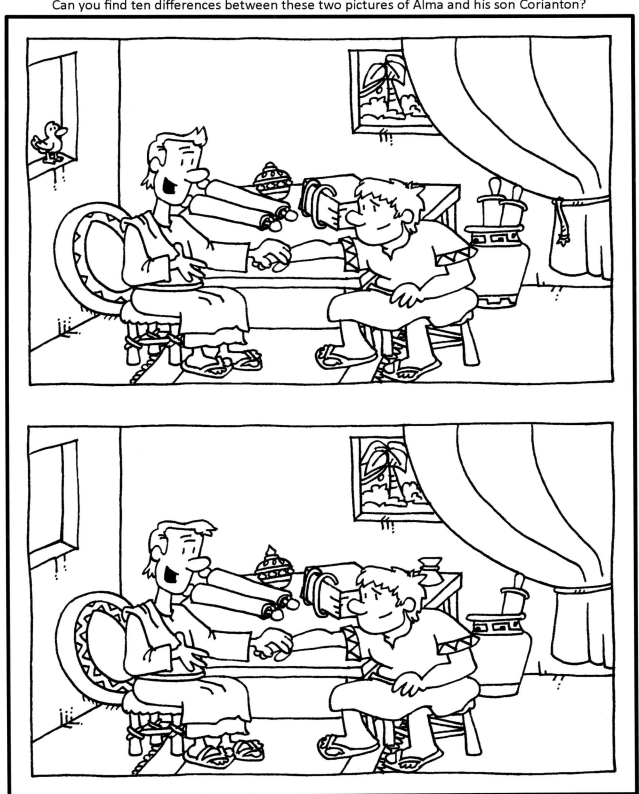

BRIGHAM YOUNG SILHOUETTE

Which of the five shadows below is an exact match of the picture of Brigham Young?

(A)

(B)

(C)

(D)

(E)

SINGING SERVICES

These children are serving by singing for others. Match the notes with the correct letters and fill in the blanks to find what the Apostle James said in the Bible about this type of service (see James 1:27). Then see if you can find the hidden letters in the picture that spell JAMES.

E G I L N O P R U

LEHI'S VISION

According to the Spirit of the Lord, what represents the Son of God in Lehi's vision? To find out, match each square below with the corresponding square in the picture. Then write the letter to the left of the square followed by the letter above the square in the spaces provided.

DEACONS' RESPONSIBILITY

Identify one of the most critical responsibilities of the Aaronic Priesthood by crossing out the letter under each deacon who's tie has a match. Then combine the remaining letters for your answer.

_____ _____ _____ _____ _____ _____ _____ _____

NEPHI'S BOAT

Find the hidden objects in this picture.

ON THE TRAIL

Can you find ten differences between these two pictures of pioneers on the trail to Salt Lake?

SCRIPTURE POWER

Paul wrote about the blessings of the scriptures in his epistle to the Romans. Find the chapter and verse of his message by first finding the two images below that are a perfect match and then recording their numbers. (Hint: the larger number is the chapter.)

ROMANS CHAPTER _____ VERSE _____

FAMILY REUNION

Thanks to the temple, this family has something better to look forward to than a pan of brownies. To find out what, start with person "F." Notice that person "O" is wearing the same skirt. Now find out what else person "O" has in common with someone else and continue until you have used all the letters.

F O _ _ _ _ _ _ _ _ _ _ _ _ _

FAMILY HISTORY SEARCH

Finding family history names is a great Sabbath activity. Starting in the upper left corner, draw a line from each two letter bubble that spells out the phrase: "Family History-The Spirit of Elijah." When you're done, you'll be left with one photo that has not been partially crossed out. This is the ancestor you're looking for.

CARING FOR THE EARTH

In Doctrine and Covenants 104:13, the Lord commands us to carefully care for the earth. To find out what the Lord specifically calls us to be for the earth, look at the box with the objects in it. For each object, count how many are in the picture. Then match the letters from the box with numbers on the lines below.

___ ___ ___ ___ ___ ___ ___ ___
 3   6   2   7   4   5   1   8

ETHER: THE LAST JAREDITE PROPHET

Ether observed the final days of his people from a cave. Can you observe the hidden objects in this picture?

BAKING COOKIES

Visiting neighbors is a great Sunday activity. This little girl isn't just baking cookies and visiting her neighbor. Find out what else she's doing by arranging the pictures in order and writing each picture's letter after the "S" below.

HOME-CENTERED GOSPEL LEARNING

This family loves studying the scriptures together. Can you find 10 differences in these two pictures?

ALMA THE YOUNGER

The prophet Alma compared growing a testimony to growing a tree. Can you find the two identical pictures below?

PIONEER SILHOUETTE

Which of the five shadows below is an exact match of the picture of the handcart pioneers?

(A)

(B)

(C)

(D)

(E)

TITHING PAYMENT

This little girl needs to deliver her tithing to the bishop. Can you help her make it to the front of the chapel to deliver it to him? Once you've done that, count the number of hymnbooks in the chapel.

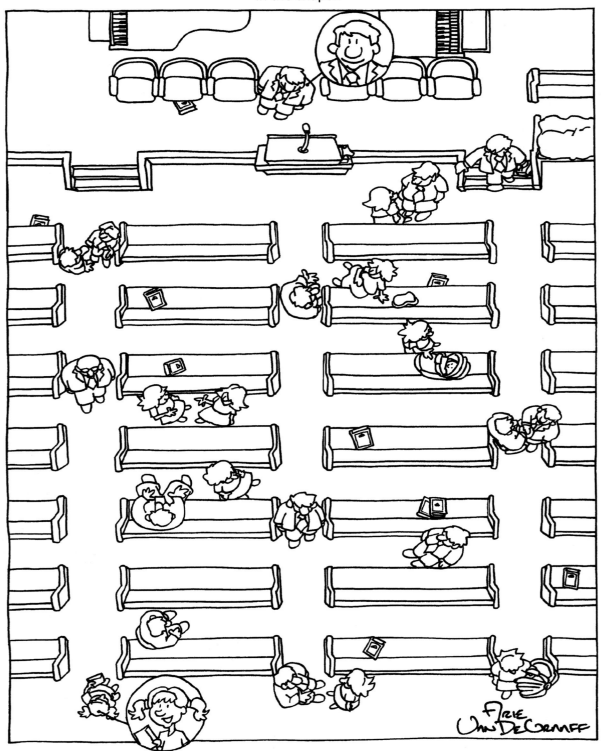

FAMILY PHOTO TIC-TAC-TOE

Can you find something the family photos in each vertical, horizontal, and diagonal set have in common?
(Hint: in the middle row, each person is wearing an apron.)

SATURDAY IS A SPECIAL DAY

One way to keep the Sabbath day holy is to prepare for it on Saturday. This family wishes they had gotten themselves and their home ready for Sunday. Can you help them find the objects they are missing?
Also see if you can find and circle eight missing crayons.

PRAYER OF THANKS

The scriptures teach us that we should thank God in all things. Try to find the thing this girl has thanked Heavenly Father for twice during her prayer. Then count the number of living things, the number of foods, and the number of round things she is thankful for.

FAMILY HIKE

Some activities (like this family hike) are best done on days other than Sunday. Find the hidden objects in the picture.

PUBLISHING THE BOOK OF MORMON

Hyrum Smith, Joseph Smith, and Oliver Cowdery admire the published Book of Mormon. Which two images below are exactly the same?

MOUTH OF TWO OR THREE

Missionaries' testimonies, the Book of Mormon and the Bible, and Paul's words to the Corinthians all are an example of a law referenced in the scriptures. Find out the name of that law by identifying something each missionary has in common with another. Start with the Elder in the upper left corner. He has the same satchel as the Elder next to him. Now find something that missionary has in common with another. Record each missionary's letter below until you've spelled out the answer.

W I __ __ __ __ __ __ __ __ __ __

WALKING TO CHURCH

Find the missing items this family will use at church in the picture below.

BOOKMARK	CTR RING	FRIEND MAGAZINE
GLASSES	HYMNBOOK	MANUAL
NOTEBOOK	PEN	PENCIL
SCRIPTURE BAG	TITHING SLIP	WATCH

EXAMPLES OF THE BELIEVERS

Sometimes missionaries can feel uncomfortable. Paul taught a young missionary named Timothy to "let no man despise thy" what? Find out by identifying the five shadows that are not exactly right. Their letters spell out your answer.

LOST COMPANION

The missionary at the bottom of this picture is looking for his companion. Each missionary in the picture is wearing a tie that matches his companion's tie.
Find the elder without a matching tie, and you will find the missionary's companion.

28

EARLY GENERAL CONFERENCE

Today General Conference is broadcast to millions, while the first General Conference was attended by just 27 people! Can you find the hidden objects in this picture of an early General Conference?

SCRIPTURE HERO CROSSWORD

Complete the crossword puzzle by writing the name of each scripture hero in the matching boxes.

Scripture Heroes:

Abinadi
Alma
Benjamin
Daniel
Moroni
Peter
Rebekah

PLAYGROUND QUESTION

Does the world seem big and confusing? There's a way to find help whenever you need it!
Find each of the 6 squares below in the bigger picture. Then write the letter to the side and to the
top of that square (the side letter first, then the top letter) in the space provided below.

L   Y   T   R   R   D   V   Y

P
E
A
N
A
Y
E
S

_ _ _ _ _ _   _ _ _ _

ASK THE MISSIONARIES

President Nelson encouraged us during the October 2012 General Conference to "Ask the missionaries! They can help you!" Find the missionary companionship in your area by starting at the upper left-hand corner and draw a straight line from each two-letter bubble that spells out the phrase "Ask the missionaries! They can help you!" When you're done, the two missionaries who don't have a line through them are your missionaries!

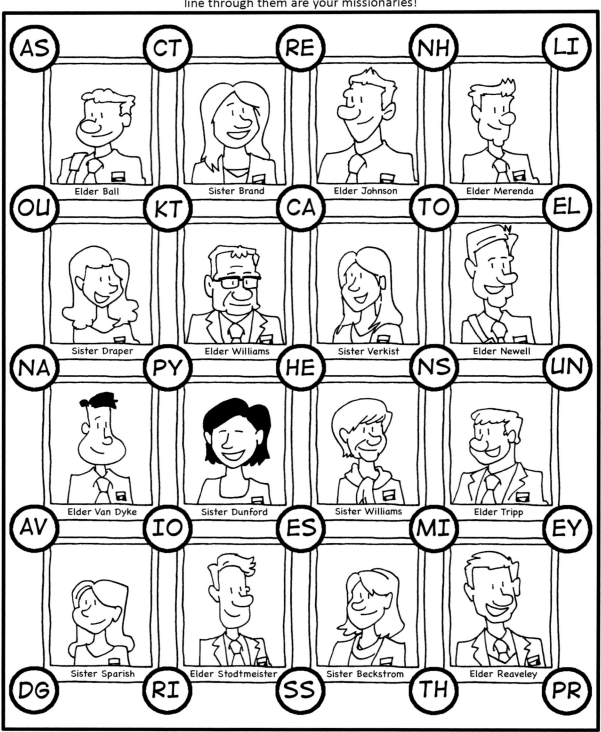

EXAMPLES OF FAITH

Linda K. Burton referred to female examples of faith using a particular scriptural phrase during the April 2017 General Conference. Discover that phrase by writing the names of the examples of faith below in the space provided and then unscrambling the circled letters at the bottom of the page. (Hint: see Luke 24:22)

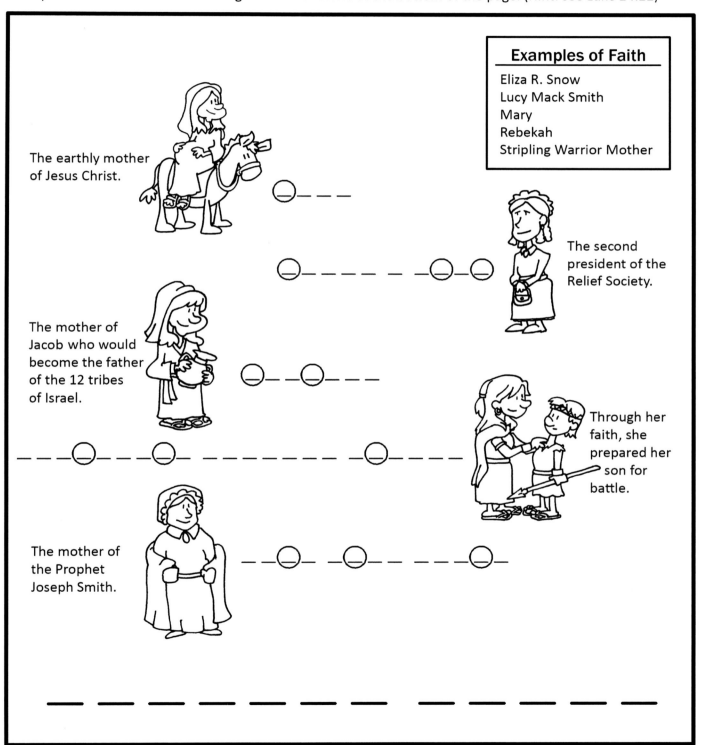

Examples of Faith

Eliza R. Snow
Lucy Mack Smith
Mary
Rebekah
Stripling Warrior Mother

The earthly mother of Jesus Christ.

The second president of the Relief Society.

The mother of Jacob who would become the father of the 12 tribes of Israel.

Through her faith, she prepared her son for battle.

The mother of the Prophet Joseph Smith.

TEMPLE OPEN HOUSE

Find the hidden objects in this picture of a temple open house.

CHRISTMAS CAROLERS

Can you find ten differences between these two pictures of carolers at Christmastime?

CAPTAIN MORONI SILHOUETTE

Which of the five shadows below is an exact match of the picture of Captain Moroni?

(A)

(B)

(C)

(D)

(E)

TEMPLE WORK MATCH

In the New Testament, one of Jesus Christ's original apostles taught about missionary work for the dead. Find out who by using the clues found on each temple-ready card to match each card's letter with the photos below.

MISSIONARY MAZE

Help the Sister Missionaries find their investigator. Then see if you can find the path to the angry dog, empty mailbox, and slammed door.

LIGHT OF THE WORLD

What are you supposed to be when Jesus asks you to be "the light of the world"? Find out by counting the number of each light source in the box and then adding each light source's letter with its number below.

__	__	__	__	__	__	__
3	1	4	5	6	2	3

LED BY THE SPIRIT

Nephi showed great faith in returning to Jerusalem after failing twice to obtain the Brass Plates. Find the hidden objects in the picture below.

CHRISTMAS PLAY

This Christmas play shares a special message. To solve the puzzle and learn the message, start with person P. Notice that person E is wearing the same hat. Write P and E in the first two spaces. Then find who has something in common with person E. Keep going until you've used all the letters.

P E __ __ __ __   __ __   __ __ __ __ __ __

MIXED-UP TOOLS

These children have taken to heart Paul's counsel to "be not weary in well doing." Find out how by writing the letter next to the boy at the fence in the first space below. Then find the child who needs his tool and write the letter next to that child. Continue until you've spelled out the answer.

HANNAH AND SAMUEL

Hannah promised the Lord to dedicate her son to Him should the Lord help her have a son. Hannah kept her promise to the Lord and Samuel would grow into a great prophet. Discover what gospel principle Hannah faithfully displayed by matching each square below with the corresponding square in the picture. Next write the letter to the left, then the letter above those squares in the space provided.

SISTER MISSIONARY SILHOUETTE

Which of the five shadows below is an exact match of the picture of the sister missionaries?

(A)

(B)

(C)

(D)

(E)

FAMILY FUN

Some activities are best performed on another day rather than Sunday. Can you find 10 differences in the pictures of this family campout?

MISSION CALL

This family is finding out where their daughter and sister is going on her mission.
Can you find the hidden objects in the picture?

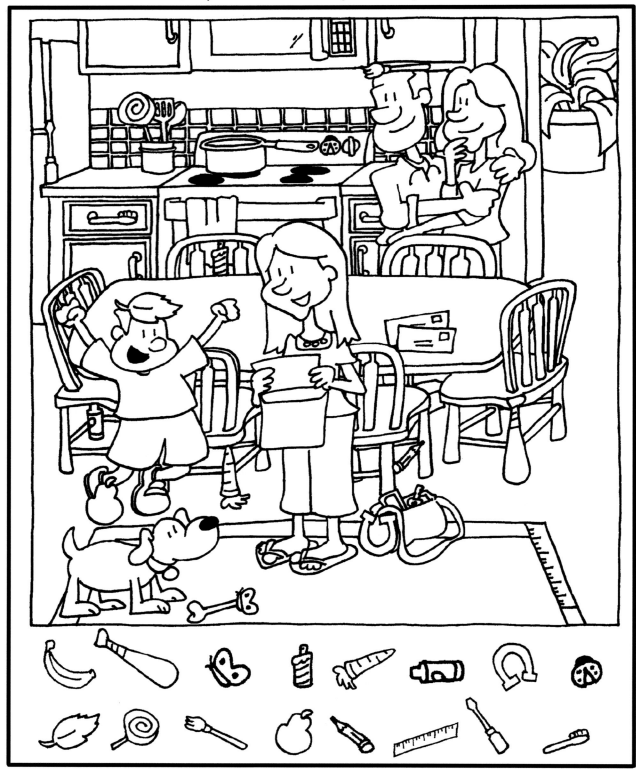

QUEEN ESTHER

Brave Queen Esther risked her life to save the Jews in her Kingdom. Can you find two pictures that are exactly the same?

BAPTISM FAMILY HOME EVENING

For Family Home Evening, this family is learning about baptism. See how many objects you can identify that start with the letter "B" in this picture.

PRIMARY CLASS TIC-TAC-TOE

Can you find something the children in each vertical, horizontal, and diagonal set have in common?
(Hint: in the top row all the boys are wearing ties.)

3 NEPHI CHAPTER 1

Why are some of these people happy and others sad? Find out what heavenly sign just took place by matching each square below with the corresponding square in the picture. Then write the letter to the left and the letter above those squares in the space provided.

CONFERENCE CENTER

This little girl is excited to see General Conference at the Conference Center. Now see if you can find all the hidden objects in this picture.

FAMILY HOME EVENING LESSON

Find 10 differences between these two pictures of a Family Home Evening lesson.

CHURCH PAGEANT

Help the Sister Missionaries find three people who want to learn more about the Church. See if you can find five members of the pageant in the audience as well.

ENOS PRAYING

Enos prayed for a day and a night for himself, his people, and his enemies. Find the two pictures that are exactly the same.

EASTER EGG HUNT!

Help these kids find 10 hidden Easter eggs. Then find 10 more hidden objects.

SCRIPTURE MOTHERS

Match each scripture mother with her silhouette, based on the description given.

Bravely allowed her four sons to return to a hostile land to retrieve the Brass Plates. (1 Nephi 5)

The mother of Jacob who would become the father of the 12 tribes of Israel. (Genesis 24)

The mother of the Prophet Joseph Smith. (JSH 1)

Mary   Lucy Mack Smith   Rebekah   Ruth   Sariah   Eve

The mother of all living. The first woman on the earth. (Genesis 2)

She cared for her mother-in-law Naomi and would go on to be the great-grandmother of King David. (Ruth 1)

The mother of Jesus Christ. (Luke 2)

WATCHING GENERAL CONFERENCE

The first weekend in April and October, people all over the world gather as families to watch General Conference. Can you find 10 differences in the pictures below?

BOOK OF MORMON PAGEANT

These Primary children are putting on a Book of Mormon Pageant. See if you can find the hidden objects in this picture.